CORNWALL
RUGBY CHAMPIONS

Also by Colin Gregory

Historic Inns of Cornwall
A Hundred Years of Cornish Photographs

CORNWALL
RUGBY CHAMPIONS
—— Colin Gregory ——

Published in association with the
Western Morning News and *Evening Herald*

PARTRIDGE PRESS

LONDON · NEW YORK · TORONTO · SYDNEY · AUCKLAND

TRANSWORLD PUBLISHERS LTD
61–63 Uxbridge Road, London W5 5SA

TRANSWORLD PUBLISHERS (AUSTRALIA) PTY LTD
15–23 Helles Avenue, Moorebank, NSW 2170

TRANSWORLD PUBLISHERS (NZ) LTD
Cnr Moselle and Waipareira Aves,
Henderson, Auckland

Published 1991 by Partridge Press
a division of Transworld Publishers Ltd

A catalogue record for this book is available from the
British Library

ISBN 185225 1662

Typeset in 12.5/14 Erhardt by
Falcon Typographic Art Ltd, Edinburgh & London
Printed in Great Britain by
M & A Thomson Litho Ltd, Glasgow, Scotland

This volume is dedicated to the thousands who were at Twickenham on 20 April 1991, or who greeted the team back into Cornwall the following day. We will never forget, because 'We were there.'

Acknowledgement

Many people who deserve my thanks are mentioned in this book, from officials to players, but I will add to them the Cornish supporters who made the away games such good fun, and especially Nigel Davies who shared the momentous trip to snowbound Newbury.

Contents

The author, Colin Gregory. (*Colin Higgs*)

Foreword

David 'Benjie' Thomas has been Cornwall's coach since 1975 and coached the team for the ADT County Championship final, 1991.

I was delighted when Colin asked me to write a foreword to this book on Cornish rugby. Over the past seasons Colin has been close to the Cornish squad, and his reports in the *Western Morning News* have reflected his great love of Cornwall and of its rugby in particular. He understands only too well the fierce patriotism that Cornish people hold for their beloved county.

His task of writing on the Cornish game is an immense challenge. We have a proud history stretching back so many years, and encompassing great games, fine players and able administrators. Cornwall has contributed a great deal to English rugby, and this was no more evident than in April when Twickenham was filled to capacity. What other county could do that?

The bench marks that will stand out are obviously 1908 and 1991, and in mentioning these one can only think of Bill Osborne, who saw both. I wonder if there could have been any comparison between the two sides? Both brought glory to the Duchy and its supporters.

The exploits of our team this season have raised everyone's morale, and together with Trelawny's Army, have gained the respect of everyone far and wide. Our musical accompaniment may be bizarre, but it only goes to show that we in the gold and black are different from 'them across the Tamar'.

Thank you Colin for your support, and for a book which I am sure will bring pleasure to many.

David Thomas
May 1991

1

Return in Triumph

Something happened on 20 April 1991 that united the people of Cornwall in a way nothing had done since the days of Bishop Trelawny, hundreds of years before.

The Cornwall rugby team won the ADT County Championship of England by beating Yorkshire by 29 points to 20 at Twickenham in front of a capacity crowd of 57,000 people, the majority of them Cornish. It was a victory which will always be remembered with pride not only by those who were fortunate enough to be there, but also by people who watched the game on television, listened to it on the radio or read the newspaper accounts.

It made us all proud. Not just those of us who have been supporters of Cornwall's rugby team for years, or even those who had simply been following in the past few glory years when the Twickenham final has been reached twice in three seasons.

It went much further than that. Grandmothers who had never seen a rugby match in their lives switched on their sets to see how 'our boys' were getting on, children were getting excited in the run-up to the game, fans of other sports were proud to don the black-and-gold favours and travel to rugby's headquarters to watch a different-shaped ball. Ex-patriot Cornish-

men came home from abroad, trains and coaches filled the routes to London, and even a jet plane and a helicopter were called in to get people to Twickenham.

After years in which life had not gone well for the Cornish – mines ceasing production, factories closing, traditional skills and industries dying – the victory at Twickenham was at last something everyone could cheer about. So often the fate of the people of Cornwall seemed to be dictated by people elsewhere. Grants to the mines cut by Westminster, subsidies cut by Europe, decisions on Cornish jobs and life dictated from far away.

On 20 April a squad of twenty-one Cornish rugby players and nearly 40,000 supporters, all backed by hundreds of thousands watching and listening at home, had the satisfaction of going to London and coming back winners. At last, we had shown them and we were the champions.

Of course, the euphoria which greeted the resulting victory was based on the Cornish team's success, but passion and enthusiasm were also stoked up by the way it was done. Losing 16–3 with sixteen minutes to go, playing against the wind and losing our captain with a ligament injury, Cornwall appeared to be dead and buried. The team came back from the jaws of defeat to score 26 points on the trot to take the county championship trophy from the hands of the Cornwall Rugby

Glyn Williams, who took over the captaincy of the side when Chris Alcock left the field injured, holds the ADT Security Systems County Championship trophy. (*Colin Higgs*)

Glyn Williams with some of the key men in Cornish rugby. They are, *left to right*, Dr Victor Phillips honorary secretary, Bill Bishop, Cornwall's representative on the RFU, and C.R. 'Bonzo' Johns, chairman of selectors. (*Colin Higgs*)

Football Union (CRFU) patron, the Duke of Edinburgh.

Those final few minutes which saw that dramatic turnaround are what most people remember, but what brought them about goes back a long way. The winning of the county championship in 1991 was linked to the first and only previous time Cornwall had taken the title, in 1908, in that it had always been the ultimate goal for any team in the black and gold.

In this story we will start at the end and then go back to the beginning, which for these purposes is that 1908 final. The end, of course, was that magnificent homecoming for the team as they arrived back in Cornwall by coach on the day after they had won the championship.

The homecoming started even before the team reached Cornwall when they stopped

for a celebratory lunch at Lewdown, over the border in Devon, with Cornish comedian Jethro who has a roadhouse and restaurant there. The road was lined with cheering supporters from the Cornish border at Polson Bridge right down to Truro, where thousands of people were gathered in the centre for a welcome home the like of which Cornwall had never seen before. Even the soldier statue on Truro's war memorial in Boscawen Street was wearing a bobble hat and scarf and holding a black-and-gold umbrella.

To quote my *Western Morning News* colleague, Robert Jobson, who was there

Even Truro's war memorial was in gold and black for the victorious homecoming. (*Colin Higgs*)

The team, wives and girlfriends, and officials arrive in Truro on an open top bus to a tumultuous welcome. (*Colin Higgs*)

amongst a sea of fans – estimated to number up to 10,000 – packed into the centre of Truro, the emotional welcome capped 'an incredible weekend of drama, despair and triumph.'

A chanting mass, clad in the county's gold-and-black colours, cheered and sang their hearts out as the Cornish squad arrived back aboard an open-topped bus. 'The people of Cornwall turned out not just to celebrate a rugby win, but to marvel at the true grit of their team which turned almost certain defeat into victory,' said the newspaper.

Trelawny's Army, the label that Cornwall's loyal and fanatical supporters had acquired over the previous few seasons as interest in rugby and the county team grew, was there to welcome home its heroes just as it had supported them on the road to the final and almost willed them on to that incredible victory.

It was a great day to follow the greatest day. What led to it was a lot of dedication by players, officials and everyone with an interest in Cornish rugby to emulate that great season of 1908, when Cornwall were first champions of all England.

2

1908 and All That

From the days when the Cornwall Rugby Football Union was formed in 1883 at Truro, one of the objects has been to find a team to take on other counties and, preferably, beat them.

The second objective took over a year to come to fruition because, after home and away defeats against Devon in 1883 and January 1884 the Cornish side had their first taste of victory on 2 December 1884, at Redruth Recreation Ground, defeating their rivals from across the Tamar by a goal and two tries to a try. The try, of course, was then worth just 3 points, making a score of 11–3.

It took much longer to win a county championship match. Cornwall entered the competition in 1892, three years after its inception, and lost both games, against Gloucestershire and Devon, without scoring a single point. It was another eight years before Cornwall savoured the taste of victory in the championship with a two-try 6–0 win over Somerset at Redruth.

It was the first step of success which led to Cornwall's greatest triumph, the winning of the county championship in the season 1907–8. It was a triumph never achieved again, although there have been some very near misses, until 20 April 1991.

The first match of that season, against Somerset at Taunton in November 1907 attracted 3,000 spectators and resulted in a clear victory by 25 points to 6. It was tougher against a strong set of Devon forwards at Plymouth and Cornwall lost 17–8. However, a remarkable recovery in the match against Gloucestershire at Redruth which ended 34–10 saw Cornwall through to two play-offs. This time they beat Devon 21–3 and Gloucestershire 15–3 to earn a semi-final against Middlesex at Redruth.

Middlesex, regarded as public school and university toffs by the Cornish, arrived with a weakened side to play in front of a 9,000 crowd at Redruth and conceded five tries in a 19–3 defeat.

The final was to be against England's strongest county side, Durham, making their ninth successive appearance, on 28 March 1908, at Redruth. Conversations in Cornwall in the weeks leading up to the final were of little else.

Newspaper reports of the time said, 'Every train that arrived poured forth its hundreds to swell the throng, and just before the kick-off there were fully 15,000 present, and this number increased to 17,000 during the match. Every town in the Duchy sent its supporters, while excursions from Devon also brought large contingents.'

Cornwall had some legendary names. There was Bert Solomon, who once played for England when they defeated Wales at Twickenham and then is reputed to have announced 'I've finished.' He is said to have been able to feint a pass so successfully that threequarters outside him would dive for the line convinced they had received a pass while he, still in possession, was touching down under the posts. At full-back was England player John Jackett who in his young days was reputed to have practised at Falmouth rugby ground by putting pails around the line and touch-kicking the ball into them.

Durham had five internationals in the pack alone, and the teams lined up as follows:

Cornwall
E.J. Jackett (Leicester)
B. Bennetts (Devon Albion)
B. Solomon (Redruth)
F. Dean (Albion)
J. Jose (Albion)
T.G. Wedge (St Ives)
J. Davey (Redruth)
J.G. Milton (Camborne School of Mines)
A.J. Wilson (Camborne School of Mines)
F. Jackson (Leicester)
R. Jackett (Falmouth)
A.J. Thomas (Albion)
R. Davey (Redruth)
T. Lawry (Redruth)
N. Tregurtha (St Ives)

Durham
D. Ellwood (Hartlepool Rovers)
H.K. Imrie (Durham City)
C. Adamson (Durham City)
P. Watson (Hartlepool Rovers)
A.V. Emerson (West Hartlepool)
J. Thompson (Hartlepool Rovers)
J. Knaggs (Hartlepool Rovers)
F. Boylen (Hartlepool Rovers)
S. Brittain (Hartlepool Rovers)
G.E. Carter (Hartlepool Rovers)
H. Havelock (West Hartlepool)
J. Duthie (Winlaton Vulcans)
G. Summerscales (Durham City)
W.H. Phillips (Durham City)
T. Hoggarth (Hartlepool Rovers)

In a fashion which was repeated eighty-one years later in the 1989 final between the two counties at Twickenham, there was once again tremendous friendly rivalry between the supporters. The Durham men in 1908 tied a monkey mascot to one cross bar while the Cornish hitched up a pasty to the other.

We know the result, Cornwall won by 17 points to 3, scoring one goal and four tries to a solitary penalty goal. Cornwall opened the scoring with a try by Solomon, and later set up another.

'The visiting threes looked dangerous, when Solomon suddenly whipped in and intercepted. Putting on top speed, he went into Ellwood and gave to Bennetts, who raced over and planted behind the posts, Jackson goaling amidst enthusiasm.' Adamson gave Durham their only score with a penalty goal, to make it 8–3 at half time.

Shortly into the second half it was that man Solomon again. Receiving from Davey, he galloped for the line with Bennetts in close attendance. A few yards from the line Solomon feinted to send him in, but then dived over himself with three men on him.

The Cornish forwards took over the game and, with their protection outside-half, Wedge, and scrum-half, Davey, they had plenty of space. A clean heal saw Wedge feed 'Maffer' Davey for try number four and later pass to Nick Tregurtha for the fifth.

The Cornish were ecstatic. The streets of Redruth were choked as the celebrations continued while the teams went off to the Masonic Hall at Redruth for a complementary dinner. The soup, I notice from the menu, was 'Consomme aux Durhams' or 'Potage aux Cornwalls'.

The victory also inspired the printing of some memorial cards and poetry, with one proclaiming:

It was a famous victory, proclaim it all
   around
How Cornwall beat Durham at the
   Recreation Ground
That Durham tried their best to everyone
   was plain
But the Pasties were too hard for them,
   their efforts were in vain.

That victory brought an honour to Cornwall which is unlikely ever to be repeated. As national rugby champions they were invited to represent England in the Olympic Games seven months later at the White City in London. Playing for the Olympic title, Cornwall lost heavily 32–3 but each player was presented with an Olympic cap. Whether every member of the team was also presented with an Olympic silver medal is a matter of conjecture. Some say they all received medals, others say there was just one which was drawn for by the players and was won by T.G. Wedge. It is still on show at the St Ives clubhouse.

The county championship and an Olympic medal in one year, what an achievement. Cornwall waited eighty-three years for the championship to return, but the opportunity for an Olympic place is unlikely to occur again. As an interesting aside, Devon also appeared in the Olympics. The appearance by the Devon County Wanderers in Paris in 1900 was the only occasion cricket was included in the Olympic Games, but that's another story.

Cornwall had high hopes of repeating their county championship success in the following season. They reached it, meeting Durham again but this time at West Hartlepool. They lost 12–0, and although they got to the final hurdle on four further occasions it was not until 1991 that the trophy came back across the Tamar.

Cornwall lost in Yorkshire in 1928, in Warwickshire in 1958, at home to Lancashire in 1968 and at Twickenham to Durham in 1989. The captain, Grant Champion, said after that 13–9 defeat, 'We'll be back,' and he proved to be right.

Another man who made a return to Twickenham which is unlikely ever to be equalled was Cornish supporter Bill Osborne, aged 103. Bill became the only man alive to see Cornwall win two county championships. 'I wouldn't have missed it for the world. It is worth living 103 years for,' was his reaction to the 1991 victory.

'I have never seen anything like it and shall never see anything like it again. I have had a wonderful time. I didn't feel the cold nor my age. The excitement overcame all that,' he said.

Bill, a former engineer from the old mining village of Four Lanes, near Redruth, was a young man at Cornwall's previous championship victory at the nearby Recreation Ground in 1908.

He went to Twickenham for the 1989 final and was in the grandstand for the Yorkshire game. He admitted he had his doubts about ever seeing Cornwall repeat their 1908 victory as the first half drew to a close. 'I could see the game and was able to follow it, but I didn't enjoy the first half and wished I had stayed at home,' he said.

As Cornwall hit back his spirits rose. 'Someone next to me got so excited he threw his arms around me every time Cornwall scored.'

When Cornwall turned the game around to snatch victory, Bill was glad he had made the trip. 'It was worth going just to see the crowd on the pitch after the game. There must have been 12,000 of them on the field. All that black and gold.'

His grandson Barrie said, 'He remembered seeing Cornwall score the winning try in the corner at Redruth in 1908 but said it was nothing compared to this win.'

A real return in triumph. Bill Osborne, 103, who saw Cornwall win the championship in 1908, was at Twickenham in 1991 with his seventy-five-year-old son, Frank. 'It was worth waiting a hundred and three years for,' he said. (*Mike Cox*)

The People at the Helm

Before we start on Cornwall's path to the final in terms of matches, it is worth looking at the selection committee which put in miles of travelling and hours of watching players who had been tipped as having the skill to play for the county.

Chairman Charles Robert Johns, better known as 'Bonzo', is supremely fitted to chair a panel of county selectors. Bonzo has made more appearances for Cornwall than any other player, eighty-eight times between 1954 and 1969, closely followed by Peter Hendy, eighty-six appearances, and Brian 'Stack' Stevens with eighty-three.

Chairman of the selectors for four years, Bonzo played at Twickenham six times in a career spanning twenty-one years, all spent with Redruth after making his début against Camborne when only sixteen. He was first a coalman, working on Saturday mornings

C. R. 'Bonzo' Johns, chairman of selectors, on his milkround in Redruth. (*Colin Higgs*)

The three Bs. *Left to right*, Benjie, Bonzo and Brian Jenkin (*John Chapman*)

then going home for his 'bath and pasty' before playing rugby. He is now a milkman, with an undiminished enthusiasm for rugby and life in general.

Bonzo played in two county finals, against Warwickshire at Coventry in 1958 and against Lancashire at Redruth in 1969. He is regarded as the finest uncapped Cornishman, having played for the Barbarians, appeared in three England trials and having been invited to tour with the British Lions in South Africa and with England in New Zealand. He could not accept a place on either tour because, as a young man just out of the Army in the days of ten shillings-a-day allowances for players, he could not afford to take time off work.

Straightforward but always good humoured, I saw Bonzo at the last training session at Bracknell on the night before the Yorkshire game and asked him what the Cornwall squad would have to eat before the big match. 'We'll have soup and sandwiches laid on for them but a lot will be so nervous they won't touch the sandwiches,' he said.

Bonzo used to tuck in before a game. 'I always used to have a proper meal. I would have soup, then egg, steak and chips, followed by a sweet and a schooner of sherry before I played a big game,' he said.

Coach David 'Benjie' Thomas has been sixteen years in the job, following ten years as a player during which he made twenty-one appearances for Cornwall. A school-teacher at Penryn, Cornwall captain Chris Alcock described Benjie in the CRFU's publication *The Path to the Final* as the players' man who is dedicated to the cause. 'He eats, sleeps and even skis county rugby . . . his greatest asset is, without doubt, to motivate men, not only on but also off the pitch,' wrote the skipper.

The reference to skiing came partly because of the epic journey Benjie made to reach the 1989 final. He had booked a skiing holiday in the French Alps the previous year way before Cornwall looked likely to reach the final against Durham, and had to make an epic journey by car, coach and aircraft to get back to London the day before the game to take Cornwall's final training session.

At 4 a.m. on the morning before the game he was picked up by car near the Swiss

The coaching never stops. David 'Benjie' Thomas in action at Redruth.

border and driven 100 miles to Grenoble where he caught a flight to Orly airport in Paris. After checking out he took a bus across Paris to Charles de Gaulle airport where he picked up a British Airways flight to Heathrow. He was then met by car and driven down to Bracknell Rugby Club where he took the Cornwall squad for their final session.

Brian Jenkin, of Hayle, one of Cornwall's most exhilarating outside-halves and with forty-five appearances between 1972 and 1984, became a selector on the retirement of another county stalwart, Chris Durant, after the 1989 final. Former Falmouth player David Chatterton, whose son Mark came on as replacement in the final, and Launceston's Don Palmer, an astute observer of players who has nurtured talent at Launceston such as Graham Dawe and Richard

Nancekivell, also made up the selection panel. Team secretary Arthur Kemp was taken ill early in the season but happily was fit enough to be at Twickenham and was holding the trophy when the squad came back to Truro. While Arthur was out of action his post was filled admirably by Peter Andrew.

Their actions were watched and encouraged by officers who included hardworking county secretary Dr Victor Phillips, president Mike Trott, chairman Merrill Clymo, treasurer Ray Plummer and of course Bill Bishop, who represents Cornish clubs on the RFU committee and who is in charge of competitions including the county championship. These and others too numerous to mention put in hours of unpaid work which is the bedrock on which a successful team on the field is built.

The Early Season Games

The backbone of the championship-winning Cornwall side were at Twickenham for the 1989 final, either on the field for that 13–9 defeat, or on the replacements bench. With Grant Champion ruled out of early season games because of injury, the captaincy went to Chris Alcock who already had experience of leading at a high level from captaining the Royal Navy side in the Inter-Services championships. Richard Nancekivell and David Rule battled it out for the scrum-half position, Graham Dawe and Brian Andrew interchanged at hooker, mainly depending on Dawe's availability as he had also been selected for the South West in the divisional games which were played on the same day as the county championship group matches.

Wingers Barrie Trevaskis and David Weeks and centre Steve Rogers all retired from county rugby, fly-half Darren Chapman suffered a nasty knee ligament injury and Alan Buzza who had played against Durham was unavailable. No. 8 Martin Haag decided to concentrate on his blossoming career in Division One with Bath, and lock Tony Cook and flanker Adrian Curtis were on the fringes of the 1990–91 squad.

To recap, Cornwall lost the 1989 final against Durham, and in the following season a 15–15 draw with Middlesex at Redruth in the semi-final was a great disappointment because the rules say that in a draw the away side goes through to the final.

It was all so tantalizingly close to the goal of taking the county championship again after eighty-three years. What was the season 1990–91 to bring? The answer, if you had relied on performances in the friendly games, was very little.

After a successful German tour in August in which the opposition were club sides, it was down to something rather tougher at St Ives on 9 September. A very good Ontario touring side which included four Canadian internationals made Cornwall look ponderous and handed out a shock 21–12 defeat. Winger Lee Hughes scored Cornwall's try, and Billy Peters kicked the conversion and two penalties.

Changes were made for the Tamar Cup match against Devon at Plymouth and it was a typical storming Cornwall performance after a very shaky start which brought a 24–14 victory and tries from Richard Nancekivell, Andy Knowles (2) and Steve Berryman. Grant Champion celebrated his selection for the Barbarians with a conversion and two penalties.

With once-proud Gloucestershire demoted, the fixture was continued on a friendly basis and Cornwall went to Bristol on 4 November for a game which they won deservedly, 19–10. Jason Atkinson made his county début, and tries came

from Nancekivell and Stuart Whitworth, Billy Peters adding a conversion and three penalties.

The final warm-up match was against the Royal Navy at St Austell. With Chris Alcock representing the Navy, Glyn Williams took over the captaincy. Cornwall were reeling within minutes and went down heavily, 21–6, the score coming from a Keith Plummer try converted by Peters.

The Cornwall side was the bulk of the county championship squad, so things were not looking hopeful for a return to Twickenham in the 1990–91 season.

Bonzo Johns giving last-minute encouragement at the training session at Penryn on 17 April 1991. (*Colin Higgs*)

The ADT County Championship Begins

Cornwall's season in the championship, which was sponsored by ADT Security Systems, began against Hertfordshire at the Old Merchant Taylors' ground at Croxley Green, near Rickmansworth. It was all a bit out of the way, but a hard core of supporters found their way and I remember spotting a bus from Cornwall and following it. In the back of the bus was a sign which read 'Falmouth Marine Band' so I knew I was heading in the right direction.

The band alighted in a residential cul-de-sac and marched down to the ground with drums beating and kilts of the Cornish drinking tartan swaying. The people living near the staid Old Merchant Taylors'

'I hear the sound of distant drums'... the Falmouth Marine Band in fine voice at Redruth. (*Mike Cox*)

He nose how to play those drums. (*Mike Cox*)

ground had never seen anything like it.

The very start of our championship campaign did not quite match the build up. Hertfordshire were as psyched up as Cornwall and after some ragged passing, losing a strike against the head and our own lineout ball, all in the first twelve minutes, we fell behind to a penalty from their outside-half Ben Rudling. Another followed three minutes later, but things started to go right for Cornwall after twenty minutes when a Grant Champion penalty went over after hitting the upright.

Only Mark Wesson had the height to take on the Hertfordshire second row, but their drive and support play was tremendous and brought a try after twenty-five minutes. Jason Atkinson, in his first championship game, picked up from a scrum and passed

to Richard Nancekivell who sent right wing Tony Meade over in the corner. Captain Chris Alcock, whose tackling stifled the potential of the Hertfordshire backs, added another try but the homeside made it 10–13 just before half-time when seventeen-stone Saracens centre Laurence Smith crashed over in the corner with Cornish shirts hanging on to him.

This did not look a good omen for the second half, but the Cornish spirit really came into its own. The forwards pushed in the scrums and there was tremendous tackling by the backs. From No. 1 John May to No. 8 Jason Atkinson they gave everything, with flanker Adrian Bick a particularly potent force in the loose.

Tommy Bassett, recalled on the left wing after five years, not only stopped a try in the first half but scored one in the fifty-first minute. A typical Nancekivell break from a Cornish put-in in front of the posts brought the fourth try. Grant Champion kicked his third successful conversion before leaving the field with a badly cut eye.

'We showed a lot of character and a lot of spirit. It got better for us as it went on,' said captain Alcock. That was to be the story of the season.

The following week Cornwall were due to play Berkshire at Newbury, but with a thick layer of snow on the pitch and a blizzard sweeping across it the game was called off. Many of us travelled to that game, setting off on a freezing cold morning and passing vehicles abandoned in the snow on our journey to the Newbury ground.

All we got that day was a free programme and a warm welcome in the clubhouse, but that cancellation was to become more important in later months. Hooker Graham Dawe was playing for the South West Divisional team on the same Saturdays as the county championship group. Divisional players who had not played in the group were not eligible to play in the county championship, but that re-arranged game against Berkshire, which was played on 15 January, meant the former England hooker qualified for the later stages of the competition.

The team which had beaten Hertfordshire was again selected for the game against Middlesex on 15 December.

Middlesex, bedecked with players from the classy London clubs, underestimated Cornwall by a mile and came really unstuck in the sunshine at Redruth. A homegrown team from the farms of North Cornwall down to the harbour at St Ives showed the London boys something about motivation and committed rugby. From the moment Chris Alcock walked his side purposefully on to the pitch they showed concentration and a determination to win.

The 25–12 victory was revenge for the previous season when Middlesex had gone through to the final by scoring more tries in a 15–15 draw on the same ground.

Cornwall were absolute dynamite. They tackled, they chased, they ground the big Middlesex pack into the Redruth soil. Middlesex had speed outside but they could not use it as Cornwall hit them like battering rams.

Prop John May scored his first championship try after fifty-one games. Nancekivell and Billy Peters added two more, with Grant Champion celebrating the birth of his son earlier that week with two conversions and three penalties. It was one of the finest performances I had seen from a Cornish team.

Christmas came to give us a break and we were into 1991 with the prospect of the re-arranged trip to Berkshire. The Bath pair of Graham Dawe and Andy Reed were brought into the side in place of Brian Andrew and Paul Thomason for a game played in atrocious conditions.

Hundreds of supporters made the trip, and I commented at the time in the *Western Morning News* that they should have been awarded a campaign medal. A gale force wind was blowing, there was a hail storm and a downpour before the kick-off and rain threatened throughout. People sat in two stands, neither of which had a roof, or huddled around the touchline. I sheltered from the wind in front of a television crew but the team from Radio Cornwall sat facing the gale. One supporter listening to the match on the radio in the warmth of his lounge said afterwards, 'Gerry Clarke sounded so frozen that I shivered.'

The game itself gave Cornwall's supporters no reason to shiver. The forwards tied the game up from the start and Berkshire, although they showed a lot of commitment, did not get a look-in.

Middlesex v. Warwickshire, 15.12.90. Glyn Williams in possession against Middlesex. Brian Andrew and Paul Thomason, who were replacements at Twickenham, are to the right of the picture. (*John Chapman*)

Cornwall v Middlesex, 15.12.90.
Opposite: Adrian Bick frightens the opposition by pulling a face... (*John Chapman*)
Above, then he's off on a break. (*John Chapman*)

Cornwall v. Middlesex, 15.12.90. Richard Nancekivell goes between the posts for a try chased by Middlesex winger Mike Wedderburn. (*John Chapman*)

Cornwall's pack was strong enough to push Berkshire back at will. Mark Wesson and Andy Reed benefitted from the accuracy of Dawe's throwing in, and the back row was just too fast and strong for their rivals. Cornwall's only problem seemed to be the referee who kept blowing up and awarding penalties and put-ins to the homeside when they did not appear to have won them. He explained afterwards that had he not done so the match would have been so one-sided it would have been a farce.

Cornwall were 14–0 up at the interval through two tries from Jason Atkinson and one from Tommy Bassett. Grant Champion kicked one conversion, and in the second half Richard Nancekivell added a try.

An 18–0 victory put Cornwall into the semi-final with the advantage of a home game. Warwickshire, runners-up in the Northern group after losing 9–4 to Yorkshire, were to be the visitors.

With the attendance limited to 11,700 under the Safety of Sports Grounds Act, tickets went like hot cakes for the semi-final on 2 February. There was one change from the side which beat Berkshire, Mark Chatterton came in on the wing for Tommy Bassett, who had a rib injury caused by one of his own forwards running over him in a club game. This looked to be the end of thirty-four-year-old Tommy's illustrious and rejuvenated county career.

The Cornish pack laid the foundation for a famous 14–6 victory over Warwickshire, but there was also much credit for the backs who held out against a fierce Warwickshire onslaught in the first fifteen minutes of the second half. A superb team effort was evident, with the backs coming into their own

Cornwall v. Warwickshire, 2.2.91. Warwickshire going forward. (*Mike Cox*)

Cornwall v. Warwickshire, 2.2.91. Jason Atkinson getting the ball to Richard Nancekivell. (*Mike Cox*)

Cornwall v. Warwickshire, 2.2.91. *Above,* Glyn Williams getting the ball out. (*Mike Cox*)
Below, the Nancekivell try from a tapped penalty which caught Warwickshire napping. (*Mike Cox*)

Opposite: the players and crowd celebrate as Warwickshire are
beaten and Cornwall are bound for Twickenham. (*Mike Cox*)

when the pack went through a purple patch in the second half.

It was a wholehearted display, but the combination of Dawe's throwing and Wesson's jumping won the lineouts and the skills of John May and Richard Keast anchored the scrums. Nancekivell was in his element in the kick and rush, and captain Alcock once again led by example as he shrugged off knocks and bruises to tackle Warwickshire's attacks out of existence.

The match was just ninety seconds old when Grant Champion slotted Cornwall ahead with a penalty, but later both he and the Warwickshire captain Steve Thomas had little success in the swirling wind. After sixteen minutes Nancekivell hit the Warwickshire morale with a real sucker of a try. As the defenders prepared for him to pass out a penalty near their line to his waiting forwards, the scrum-half did a reverse turn and crashed over in the corner. It was an audacious move. 'If I hadn't scored I think I would have been dropped,' he joked afterwards.

Thomas kicked a penalty for Warwick-shire but Champion matched it to make the score 10–3 at half-time.

Warwickshire, spurred on by Thomas and their back row, which included England Universities captain Ian Pickup at No. 8, piled into Cornwall in the second half.

With the Cornish forwards winning no ball, the concentration was on keeping out the rampaging Warwickshire attackers. It was a credit to their character that the only reward Warwickshire gained was a penalty from outside-half Stewart Vaudin.

After fifteen minutes of soaking up the pressure Cornwall broke out again. After Adrian Bick had almost crossed the line, No. 8 Jason Atkinson gathered and went storming through with three defenders hanging on his back.

It was a match played at full speed, with referee Tony Spreadbury having to calm down tempers on several occasions. When Mr Spreadbury blew the whistle Cornish arms were raised in triumph, the crowd stood and cheered, there were men with tears in their eyes. Cornwall were at Twickenham again. We were going to be there.

The Path to the Final

The whole of Cornwall seemed to be going Twickenham-mad in the build-up to the final. With every bus and coach in the county booked to take supporters to the game, travel operators had to hire in vehicles from other parts of the country. Train excursions were organized, and even a sixty-four-seater aircraft was hired to fly supporters on the morning of the game from Newquay to Gatwick from where they would be transported to Twickenham by coach.

As the weeks passed it became increasingly clear that the 30,000 attendance of 1989, itself a county championship record, was to be surpassed. In the event 57,000 people, as many as the ground could legally hold, were at Twickenham on the day.

There were eleven weeks from the semi-final to the final and all the talk in Cornwall was about rugby. Top of the agenda was the team selection. Would they make changes? Would people who had not played in the previous games, such as Alan Buzza of Wasps, Martin Haag of Bath or even Colin Laity of Neath, be called up? It seemed unlikely Tommy Bassett would recover from his injury and be fit, so would Mark Chatterton keep his place or would the selectors look at one of the wingers used in the warm-up games such as Andy Knowles or Marcel Gomez?

We were going through the Gulf War at the time, and another fear Cornish rugby supporters had was that the captain Chris Alcock, a helicopter observer at RNAS Culdrose, would be sent out to the Middle East. In the 1989 season Richard Nancekivell had played in the group games but then lost his place to Camborne's David Rule, a more orthodox scrum-half. Would the same happen in 1991?

The players were training together regularly but going through the same jitters over selection. They all wanted to pull on that black-and-gold shirt at Twickenham, it would be the pinnacle of their rugby careers.

The agony, for most of them, was over on 25 March when Cornwall named their team, bar one position. They left the left-wing position blank in order to see if Tommy Bassett would recover sufficiently from his injury to be in the reckoning.

Yorkshire named the side which beat Middlesex in the semi-final. It included the country's deadliest place kicker, John Liley, of Leicester and England B, and a back row which had represented the Northern Division the previous season.

Meanwhile Cornish interest continued. Tremorvah Industries sold out of their replica Cornwall shirts, seats on the aircraft to Twickenham were selling out at a price of £139 and Cornish rugby scarves, hats, pullovers and other items were disappearing from the shops in a black-and-gold rush.

With eleven days to go the question

of who would play on the left wing was answered. Tommy Bassett, the St Ives pub landlord, was named in the team with Mark Chatterton as one of the replacements. As we were to witness later, Chatterton got his chance at Twickenham and was able to play a part in the victory. Bassett recovered from his injury despite suffering fluid on the lung. Selectors Don Palmer and Brian Jenkin watched both men playing for their clubs and the final decision was made after a training session at Penryn, with Mark's father, David Chatterton, taking no part in the discussion.

'It was a very hard decision and we had a long discussion before announcing it,' said chairman Bonzo Johns. 'Basically Tommy got his place on experience and his defensive play. Last night he trained like a twenty-year-old. He would not have got his place if he was not fully fit, and this should be the game of a lifetime for him.' How prophetic that statement by Bonzo turned out to be.

The team was picked, and on the Sunday before the game the squad went through their final training session in Cornwall. Chris Alcock, who had played for the Royal Navy side which lost at Twicken-ham the previous week in the inter-services championship, warned, 'Even if you are a few points down, you have never lost at Twickenham until the final whistle.'

The problem of whether the match would be televised live had been solved. TSW had made a bid to show it, but as the BBC had the exclusive contract for games at Twick-enham it was decided the game would go out on BBC South-West. A helicopter had been added to the various ways people were getting to the game: a story in the *Western Morning News* about Bude architect and choir conductor Jon Ball, who had discov-ered to his horror that the match clashed with an important wedding engagement,

led to the head of a helicopter charter firm arranging to pick him up from the church at noon to get him to the game on time.

Trelawny's Army, named after the 20,000-strong band of Cornishmen who had threat-ened to march on London to free Bishop Trelawny who was imprisoned in the Tower of London in 1688 accused of treason, was ready to march again. As Bill Bishop, Cornwall's representative on the RFU, said in 1989, 'Last one out of Cornwall switch the lights out.'

The roads from Cornwall to London were a procession of black and gold on the day of the game. Coaches, trains and cars had set off at the crack of dawn and the motorway service stations were packed with hundreds of Cornish men and women.

An invading army hit Twickenham. The pubs were packed with Cornishmen in good voice, and the atmosphere was warm and friendly, even towards Yorkshiremen. There were hundreds of children in the crowd who had been invited by the RFU as part of a promotions day, and many Cornish families took their young sons and daughters to the game. It was a lovely family occasion which the young as well as those who are older will not forget. Choirs were assembled on the terraces, the Falmouth Marine Band got their wish granted and marched on the pitch and a party from Truro Rugby Club hoisted a giant pasty on one of the crossbars.

There were many distinguished faces in the crowd. Sir Denis Thatcher, a regular holidaymaker and golfer at Trevose, took his seat and said he would be support-ing Cornwall. Sir Denis once refereed a county championship semi-final, so he knows something about rugby. Jan Harvey, from Penzance, who plays Jan Howard in *Howard's Way* was there with her close friend Stephen Yardley, who plays the noto-rious Ken Masters in the same programme.

Parties in the car park abounded. This one had beer delivered in the Cornish Brewery's van. (*John Chapman*)

This tops it all. Former Cornwall prop Allan Mitchell knows what it's like to be a member of the front-row union. (*John Chapman*)

Above, more manageable pasties fortify the Daniels family. *Right*, Car-boot gal Joanna Barrs. (*John Chapman*)

Opposite: top left, facing the game in black and gold. (*John Chapman*) *Top right*, 'Dear Bill, I bumped into Daphne on my way to Twickers.' ...this really is Sir Denis Thatcher, minus the Boss and with a snifter in hand, being interviewed by BBC Radio Cornwall's Daphne Skinnard. (*John Chapman*) *Below*, the pasty that was hung from the Twickenham crossbar is held aloft by Thomas Hill, aged four, with the help of Graham Hill, Brian Chenoweth and Milly Edwards, all from Truro. (*John Chapman*)

Sooty from Newquay says Cornwall will make a clean sweep. (*John Chapman*)

Support from the ladies, Mrs Monica Haag, Mrs Emileen Williams and Mrs Christina Stewart.
(*John Chapman*)

THE PATH TO THE FINAL 35

Even the Padstow boys made it. (*John Chapman*)

Stephen Yardley is from Yorkshire, but that did not sway Jan Harvey's loyalties to Cornwall.

Wherever you looked there were faces you knew. Jethro the Cornish comedian, politicians, county and club players from the past, friends, people you knew by sight but couln't put a name to. Martin Haag, who played in the 1989 final, was in the crowd. Glyn Williams' father had flown home from Kenya, where he was working as a chief electrical engineer, especially for the game. Some Cornishmen had flown from Canada and Australia to be there.

Lots of girls went to Twickenham, including Lisa Carter, from Wadebridge, with her mascot. (*John Chapman*)

The Falmouth Marine Band play to their biggest-ever audience. (*John Chapman*)

No one knows precisely how many of that 57,000 crowd were Cornwall supporters, but I don't think it could have been far short of 40,000. There were many watching a game of rugby for the first time in their lives, they were there simply because they were Cornish.

There was a huge roar as the Cornwall side came on to the pitch for the team photograph, the atmosphere was building up to boiling point. The Duke of Edinburgh, patron of the Cornwall RFU, took his seat, the teams came out to a tumultuous welcome. Battle was about to commence.

Right, Cornwall captain Chris Alcock leads his side on to the pitch. (*John Chapman*) *Below*, the official team picture, but superstitious John May stayed in the changing room. (*John Chapman*)

Overleaf: You can almost hear the roar.
The team lines up for the National Anthem and battle is about to commence. (*John Chapman*)

The Big Match

Cornwall 29, Yorkshire 20 (after extra time)

CORNWALL

K. Thomas (Plymouth Albion)
A. Mead (Plymouth Albion)
C. Alcock (Camborne and Royal
   Navy, Capt.)
G. Champion (Devon and Cornwall Police)
T. Bassett (St Ives)
W. Peters (St Ives)
R. Nancekivell (Northampton)
J. May (Redruth)
G. Dawe (Bath)
R. Keast (Redruth)
M. Wesson (Plymouth Albion)
A. Reed (Bath)
G. Williams (Redruth)
J. Atkinson (St Ives)
A. Bick (Plymouth Albion)

Replacements
M. Chatterton (Exeter, replaced Alcock
   55 minutes)
K. Plummer (Cleve)
S. Whitworth (Redruth)
A. Ellery (St Mary's Hospital)
B. Andrew (Camborne)
P. Thomason (Redruth)

Referee: R. Quittenton (London)
Touch Judges: F. Howard (Liverpool)
            A. Spreadbury (Somerset)

YORKSHIRE

J. Liley (Leicester)
M. Harrison (Wakefield, Capt.)
J. Georgiou (Halifax)
P. Johnson (Headingley)
E. Atkins (Harrogate)
S. Townend (Wakefield)
D. Scully (Wakefield)
J. Woodthorpe (Harrogate)
S. Cruise (Wakefield)
R. Burman (Wakefield)
I. Carroll (Otley)
S. Croft (Harrogate)
S. Tipping (Otley)
S. Bainbridge (Morley)
P. Buckton (Liverpool St Helens)

Replacements
J. Mallinder (Sale)
A. Caldwell (Harrogate)
I. Wright (Sheffield)
P. Wright (Middlesbrough)
J. Fletcher (Bradford and Bingley)
J. Chapman (Middlesbrough)

Andy Reed reaching for the sky, and getting it. (*Mike Cox*)

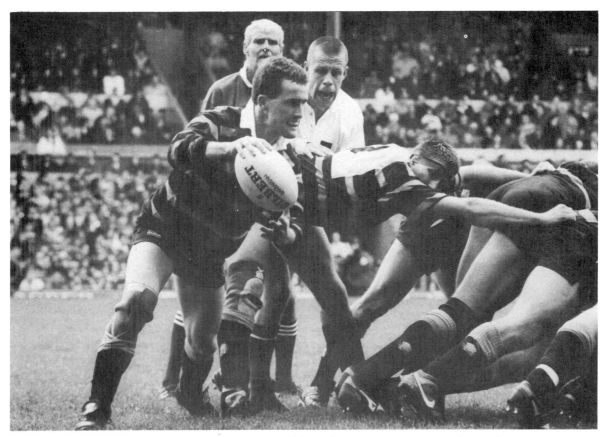

Richard Nancekivell has the ball but Yorkshire scrum-half Dave Scully is always too close for comfort. (*Mike Cox*)

This time flanker Peter Buckton puts on the pressure. (*Mike Cox*)

Opposite: Yorkshire's Sean Bainbridge gets a grip on Richard Nancekivell. (*Mike Cox*)

Yorkshire fly-half Steve Townend sends out a ball that leads to their first try from Johnson. (*Mike Cox*)

Cornwall are trailing but the supporters are still cheerful. (*Mike Cox*)

Yorkshire did the running. This is centre Jason Georgiou with the ball. (*Mike Cox*)

Basquing in the sun. This young lady did it for charity, she said. She raised £3,000 for Children in Romania, and a few cheers as well. (*Mike Cox*)

No need for streakers, the St Ives girls are here. (*Mike Cox*)

Yorkshire's Jason Georgiou slicing through again. (*Mike Cox*)

Dave Scully dives over for the try which, after Liley had converted, made it 16–3 to Yorkshire. (*Mike Cox*)

Grant Champion seems to be saying something to referee Roger Quittenton after the disputed try. It must have been something nice because the game went Cornwall's way afterwards. Lip readers tell me it was, 'He signalled a kick, you !@£$%* **&^%!!.' (*Mike Cox*)

Cornwall became county champions for the first time since 1908 in a sensational finish that is unlikely to be surpassed in another 100 years.

It was like a story from *Roy of the Rovers* transferred to the rugby field. Trailing 16–3 mid-way through the second half, playing against the wind and looking thoroughly dead and buried, Cornwall rose from the ashes to score 26 points on the trot.

A hotly-disputed try by Yorkshire, when full-back John Liley appeared to have signalled an attempt at goal, was the incident which whipped the smouldering Cornish embers into a flame of passion. With Cornwall lined up between the posts awaiting the kick, Liley tapped the ball and sent scrum-half David Scully away towards the corner. Liley then converted to make it 16–3 and it looked as though Cornwall's trip to Twickenham would end in disappointment.

Instead, they turned the game on its head to score 26 points on the trot. With just sixteen minutes to go, Cornwall came back with a try and by the end of eighty minutes had made it 16–16.

THE TURNING POINT

The second Yorkshire try in the fifty-fourth minute, which would have sunk any other team, fired Cornish pride and passion on to victory.

Liley, the Yorkshire full-back, seemed to indicate a kick at goal from penalty. Instead he tapped the ball and sent a scoring pass to unmarked scrum-half Dave Scully.

The Cornish protested, to no avail. Referee Roger Quittenton said afterwards, 'Perfectly legal. I simply asked John [Liley] if he was going for goal. His response was the perfectly legal one of tapping the ball into his hands and running it.'

The Cornish team asked touch judge Fred Howard if Liley had signalled a goal kick. Howard replied: 'I thought so.'

For the angry Cornish players it was the turning point. Flanker Glyn Williams told me, 'That was a sneaky try and it made us teasy. I thought we were gone before that, but when he scored that try everyone got so uptight we really went for it.' Lock Mark Wesson agreed. 'It was the turning point. I don't think he should have awarded that try, but afterwards we had nothing to lose.'

Hooker Graham Dawe said the Yorkshire front row surprised Cornwall early on, but the disputed try strengthened Cornwall's resolve. 'It was sheer frustration that we had not done ourselves justice. We were angry with ourselves that we were letting 40,000 people down,' said Graham. 'We thought we had blown it, but in the last fifteen minutes and into extra time we were really pumping and always going forward. We have made history and laid the ghost of 1908.'

Yorkshire captain Mike Harrison confessed, 'I'm as confused as everyone else about what happened, but I think Cornwall did exactly the same against Warwickshire.'

Grant Champion went wide with the conversion of the last try one minute from time which meant extra time of a further ten minutes each way had to be played. It was like a bonus for the Cornish supporters, and many joked afterwards that Champion had pulled it to the left to give everyone better value for money.

Cornwall then scored another 13 points in as many minutes for a victory which had, just half an hour earlier, not seemed possible.

Yorkshire came back at the end with a beautifully worked consolation try from their captain, Mike Harrison, to spread the honours all round for a wonderful game.

The feeling that the tide was turning after an abysmal fifty-five minutes spread throughout the packed stadium. The 15,000 Yorkshire supporters who had been singing 'On Ilkley Moor' with vigour were stunned into silence as their team collapsed before their eyes, steamrollered by a transformed Cornish pack.

As the roar of the Cornish supporters

This made Cornwall angry. Full-back John Liley, the highest points scorer in English rugby, takes a quick tap penalty and passes out when most thought a kick at goal had been signalled by the referee. (*Mike Cox*)

swelled, the power of their team increased. Glyn Williams, who took over the captaincy when Chris Alcock hobbled from the field with a torn ligament, inspired the players to a level where they were transformed from also-rans into The Unstoppables.

Richard Nancekivell, whose two tries which brought the scores level showed his pace off the mark, must share the accolade of Man of the Match with Glyn Williams after a shaky first half against the highly competitive Scully.

The front row of John May, Graham Dawe and Richard Keast were the corner-stone of the victory, while locks Andy Reed and Mark Wesson won good line-out balls and added real power in the scrums.

It was a team victory, with everyone playing a part. Tommy Bassett ran 50 yards across the field to throw his body behind the pack and score the first try in extra time. Who could forget his toothy grin as he emerged, with blood flowing from a cut on his head, in the ecstasy of that effort? Fly-half Billy Peters crashed over like a burly forward for the second. Grant Champion, in tears after captaining the defeated 1989 team in the final, added two conversions and three penalty goals.

Yorkshire had looked a very good side for 75 per cent of the game. The big back row of Simon Tipping, Peter Buckton and Sean Bainbridge was superb, and their backs looked razor sharp when they had the ball, but when extra time came they had hardly the energy left to stand on their feet.

Left wing Erickson Atkins was outstanding both in defence and attack, while centres Paul Johnson and Jason Georgiou made piercing runs into the Cornish defence.

It was a match which had everything: excitement and the emotional finale of a team pulling a win out of almost nothing.

The scoring went like this:

*14 minutes: Yorkshire backs move the ball across the line, from Harrison to Liley and to Johnson who scored a try. 0–4.

*26 minutes: Liley penalty from 25 metres. 0–7.

*40 minutes: Champion penalty from 20 metres. 3–7.

*42 minutes: Liley penalty from 22 metres. 3–10.

*54 minutes: Yorkshire awarded penalty. Cornwall line up thinking signal has been given for a kick at goal. Instead, Liley taps the ball to Scully who goes over for a try. Liley converts. The incident angers Cornwall. 3–16.

*64 minutes: Cornwall fighting back with a vengeance. Referee awards Cornwall three put-ins near the Yorkshire line and eventually Nancekivell burrows through for try. Champion converts. 9–16.

*74 minutes: Champion penalty, but Yorkshire look capable of soaking up the pressure. 12–16.

*79 minutes: Chatterton impeded, Cornwall run the penalty and another forward drive sees Nancekivell break away for a try. Champion's conversion attempt pulls across the posts and the game goes into extra time. 16–16.

*Extra time.

*85 minutes: Yorkshire collapse the scrum and from the penalty Champion puts Cornwall ahead. 19–16.

*89 minutes: Tommy Bassett joins the scrum and burrows through for a try as the Cornish pack roll forward. 23–16.

*92 minutes: Another rolling maul with Glyn Williams and Andy Reed leading. Billy Peters twists over to get the touch down. 29–16.

*99 minutes: Yorkshire move it wide with just 20 seconds to go. Captain Mike Harrison rounds off with a Yorkshire try. 29–20.

*100 minutes: Mr Quittenton blows his whistle. The pitch is invaded and the Cornish players carried shoulder high to mount the steps to receive the trophy from the Duke of Edinburgh.

A lone flag as Cornwall face defeat.(John Chapman)

We have to fly into them, says Glyn Williams who took over as captain. (John Chapman)

Like this. (*John Chapman*)

And this. (*John Chapman*)

The front row says now is the time for action.
(*Mike Cox*)

And the crowd says now is the time for real support. (*Mike Cox*)

Passing the ball among the forwards. Notice the Cornwall selectors and five remaining replacements on the bench. (*Mike Cox*)

Tommy Bassett stops Yorkshire and former England captain Mike Harrison. (*Mike Cox*)

Try and stop me, says Glyn Williams. (*Mike Cox*)

Peter Buckton gets a grip on John May. (*Mike Cox*)

Opposite: top, Cornwall getting so close to that line time after time. (*John Chapman*)
Bottom, it takes three Yorkshiremen to hold Andy Reed. (*John Chapman*)

Previous page: A Grant Champion penalty helps Cornwall claw back to 16–12. (*Mike Cox*)

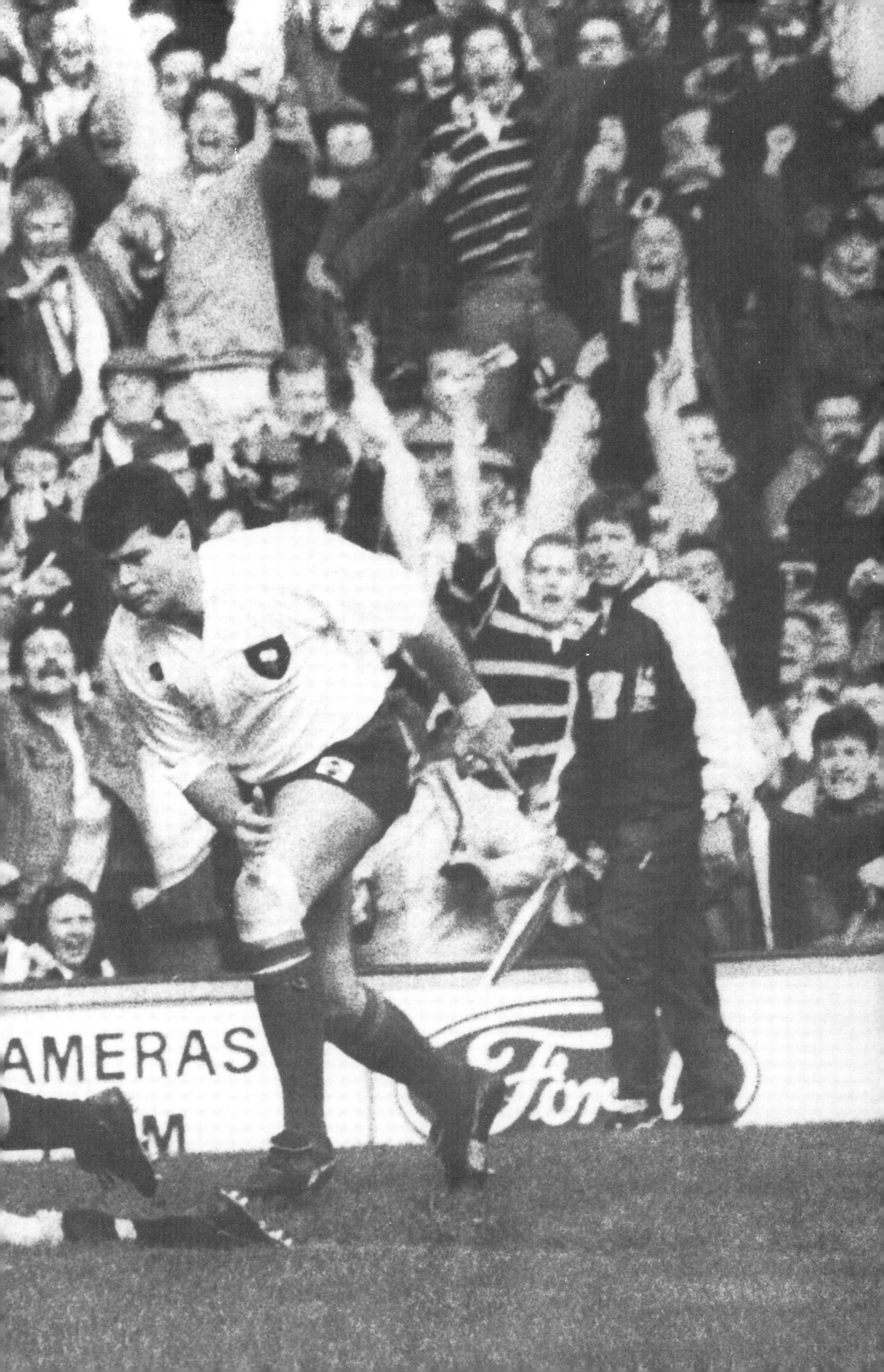
AMERAS
M
Ford

We are going to win it now. (*Mike Cox*)

Previous page: That man Nacekivell does it again
He goes through the Yorkshire cover for a try which
levels the score at 16–16. (*John Chapman*)

Opposite: What is Tommy Bassett saying to
Grant Champion? Could it be, 'Miss this one so
I can score a try in extra time'? (*Mike Cox*)

A dream comes true. Tommy Bassett is below this mêlé scoring a try which put Cornwall 23–16 ahead in extra time. (*John Chapman*)

No stopping us now. Billy Peters crashes through to make it 27–16. (*John Chapman*)

Opposite: Grant Champion adds the finishing touches. (*John Chapman*)

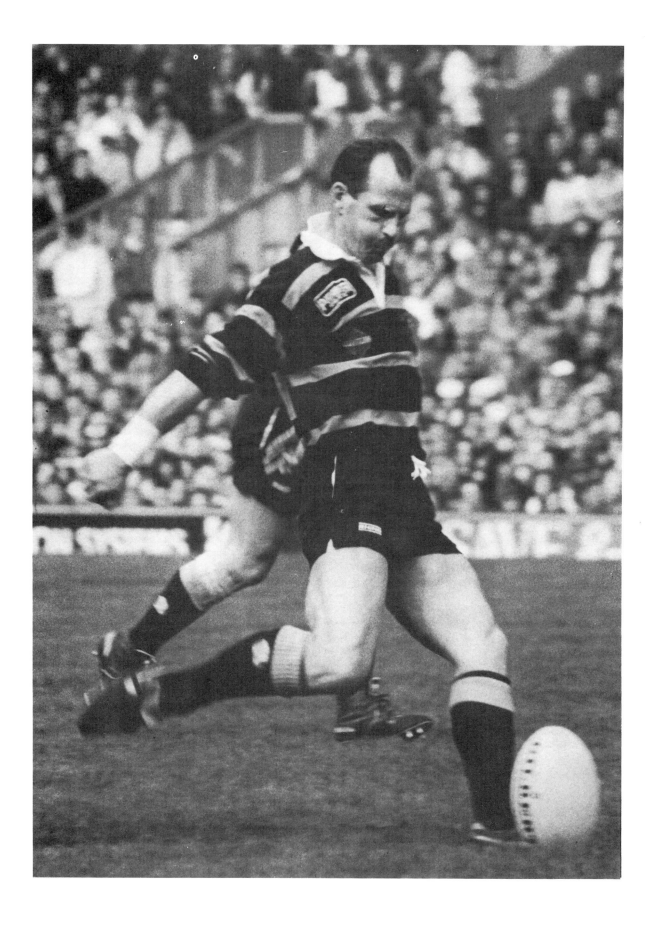

Graham Dawe
looks as if he is about to be
arrested for cruelty to Tykes
as he waits to receive
his medal. (*John Chapman*)

We have it at last.
An eighty-three-year wait to be
champions of England again is
over. (*John Chapman*)

Opposite: top, look at the
scoreboard, 29-16. Only a
Mike Harrison try to round off
the match. (*Mike Cox*) *Bottom*,
the whistle blows and we have
won. (*John Chapman*)

Andy Reed is carried aloft. (*Mike Cox*)

Opposite: top, Mark Chatterton is thrilled, and even the Duke of Edinburgh looks pleased. (*John Chapman*)
Bottom, Adrian Bick and Grant Champion hold the trophy aloft. (*John Chapman*)

Overleaf: Congratulations all round. (*John Chapman*)

8

What the Papers Said

The match, watched by 57,000 at Twickenham, was also seen live on BBC South-West by hundreds of thousands of viewers, by over a million the following day on BBC2's *Rugby Special*, and listened-to live on BBC Radio Cornwall.

It also attracted the attention of the national press in a way no county championship final had done before. Every major newspaper was represented, some by more than one journalist, and it is extremely interesting to read their comments and those of the newspaper which represents our opposition that day, the *Yorkshire Post*.

Here are some excerpts:

'A publican's hands, a policeman's boot and the massed choirs of Cornish fans drove Yorkshire to destruction in a sensational ADT county championship final at Twickenham ... Cornwall were almost dead and buried when Yorkshire, clearly the more competent side, were cruising home at 16–3. But scrum-half Dave Scully's try for Yorkshire lifted Cornwall rather than depressed them.'
– Barry Newcombe, *Sunday Express*

'The march of Trelawny's Army on Twickenham and their heroes' seizure of the County Championship have been among the most affecting spectacles the game has ever known. The crestfallen Yorkshiremen present at HQ would beg to differ, but it was an inspiration to witness a denouement

that no one would have dared to script.'
– Steve Bale, *Independent*

'Whatever else Cornwall and their joyous supporters proved at Twickenham, they deserve grateful thanks for demonstrating that intense competition, unbridled enjoyment and responsible behaviour can go hand in hand.'
– John Mason, *Daily Telegraph*

'The unforgettable sight of an entire black and yellow clan going right off their collective trolley must rank as the enduring memory of a wonderful season for English rugby.'
– Brendan Gallagher, *Daily Telegraph*

'It might not have been a classic text book game of rugby, but Cornwall will tell you what you can do with your text book. You really would have to be dead from the neck up not to have recognised yesterday as one of the most fervent and astonishing rugby occasions ever staged at Twickenham, or anywhere else for that matter ... Cornwall, apparently dead in the water early in the second half, switched on to such an extent that they came storming back, even had a kick to win it in the last second of normal time and then, like men possessed, stormed away with their first county championship win since 1908 in a tumultuous period of extra time.'
– Stephen Jones, *The Sunday Times*

'It was wild, woolly and in its way quite wonderful. Trelawny's Army had marched on Twickenham and by the end had taken it by storm, a bit like Barnum and Bailey hijacking Covent Garden. Twickenham may take some time to recover from the shock of it all, but not half as long as it will take Yorkshire to repair the damage to their shattered pride and morale.'
– Chris Rea, *Independent on Sunday*

'Who said that county rugby was a thing of the past? It never could be if the extraordinary scenes at the final of the county championship at Twickenham yesterday are anything to go by.'
– Clem Thomas, *Observer*

To end this pick of the national press, we go over to the one county where Cornwall's victory would not have been treated with elation. Bill Bridge, Sports Editor of the *Yorkshire Post*, wrote:

'Yorkshire's third, last and best try in Saturday's county championship final had all the impact of a bucket of water thrown at a fire-gutted mill.

'Cornwall fully deserved to win, despite their appalling handling, their stilted tactics and their glaring lack of pace. They won simply because they wanted victory more than a Yorkshire side in which key players did not reach peak form.'

In a separate piece the *Yorkshire Post* described the moment when Scully scored a try from Liley's tapped kick, the moment which transformed the game fourteen minutes into the second half. Cornwall's players had trooped back for what they presumed was an inevitable kick at goal . . .

'Instead Liley tapped the kick, smartly fed Scully and the try was a formality. Liley then turned Cornish anger into fury by hitting a wobbling, low conversion which gave Yorkshire six points and a 16–3 cushion. From then on the passion from the massive Cornish crowd fuelled the fire within their team and Yorkshire were simply out of the match.'

The *Western Evening Herald* also gave the game splendid coverage, with rugby writer Dick Benson-Gyles reporting:

'Cornwall rose in splendour from the dead at Twickenham to dumbfound 57,000 people and turn a dream, cherished for 83 barren years, into reality . . . Thirteen minutes into the second half and trailing hopelessly at 16–3, Cornwall seemed to be having the last rites administered with the burial just a formality to come. Then began an astonishing, fantastic resurrection.'

Describing the play, Dick Benson-Gyles went on to say: 'Anyone privileged to witness this phenomenal spectacle will have no doubt that they saw the greatest finale the county championship has ever staged, and one which is likely to have resurrected a competition many had consigned to the dustbin.'

We'll all say aye to that.

The Cornwall Squad

The Cornwall team was mainly 'home-grown'. Most of the players had come up through the Cornwall Schools or Colts system, and although some had moved away they still felt a thrill at pulling on the black-and-gold shirt.

Three, Graham Dawe, Andy Reed and Richard Nancekivell, were with Division One clubs, and four were with Plymouth Albion in Division Two. The Redruth players tasted success twice during the season as their club was promoted to National Division Three, the first Cornish club to achieve this.

CHRIS ALCOCK, captain (Camborne and Royal Navy)
Centre. Age 28, 5ft 7in, 11st 7lbs.
A Helicopter Observer Instructor at RNAS Culdrose. Captain of the Royal Navy and thirty-two caps for Cornwall before the final. Born in Warwickshire but married to a Cornish girl, Chris is a terrific tackler in defence and moves to take the high ball in attack like a guided missile.

KEVIN THOMAS (Plymouth Albion)
Full-back. Age 21, 6ft 2in, 14st.
Kevin, a fireman, joined Plymouth from Redruth. Sixteen senior caps after a distinguished career in Schools and Colts. A cool head and a long kick to touch make him sound at the back.

Captain Chris Alcock coming on to the pitch at the start of the ADT County Championship at Twickenham (*John Chapman*)

Kevin Thomas, full-back throughout the season Twickenham 1991. (*John Chapman*)

TONY MEAD (Plymouth Albion)
Right wing. Age 22, 5ft 10in, 13st 4lbs.
Tony is a policeman at Newquay and won a regular place in the side after being replacement for the semi-final and final in 1989. He played for the British Police, and the World Police XV in Ulster, 1990. Tony tackled like a demon at Twickenham.

Winger Tony Mead goes for the ball at grass-roots level. Cornwall v. Middlesex, 15.12.90. (*John Chapman*)

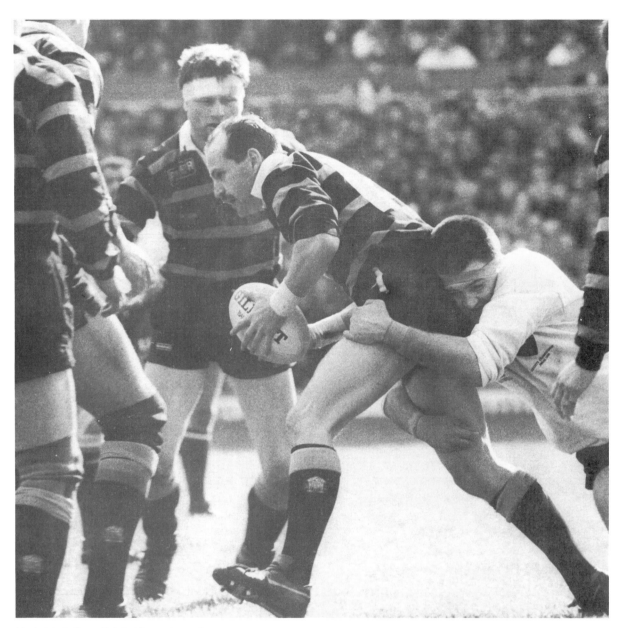

Yorkshire's Sean Bainbridge gets a grip on Grant Champion in the final. (*Mike Cox*)

GRANT CHAMPION (Truro and Devon and Cornwall Police)
Centre. Age 30, 6ft, 13st 3lbs.
A policeman at Penryn, Grant has come through the Cornwall Schools and Colts teams. He has played for the British Police and World Police, and in November 1990 played for the Barbarians in their centenary match at Bradford. A fine goal kicker and tackler, Grant could not hide his emotion when, as captain, Cornwall lost the 1989 final.

Tommy Bassett has his eye on the loose ball. Twickenham 1991. (*Mike Cox*)

TOMMY BASSETT (St Ives)
Left wing. Age 34, 5ft 11in, 12st 7lbs.
The oldest winger in town is now a publican after working as a fisherman and miner. He was a surprise but popular choice when he was recalled to the Cornwall team after a five-year gap. No one shrugs off a tackle from Tommy. A lifeboatman, he certainly came to the rescue of Cornwall.

Billy Peters on the run. Twickenham 1991.
(*John Chapman*)

BILLY PETERS (St Ives)
Fly-half. Age 23, 6ft, 13st 4lbs.
A life assurance salesman, Billy captained
Cornwall Schools and came into the senior side in the 1989 friendlies. A powerful
runner, he made what has been a problem
position for Cornwall into his own during
the 1990–91 season.

John May takes on Middlesex. Cornwall v. Middlesex, 15.12.90. ((John Chapman)

JOHN MAY (Redruth)
Loose head prop. Age 35, 5ft 10in, 15st 6lbs.
John is a farmer at St Merryn and joined Redruth from Wadebridge Camels in 1982. Fifty-three Cornish caps after début in 1983. Acknowledged as a specialist in his position, he played for the Cornwall and Devon XV against Spain in 1986.

RICHARD NANCEKIVELL (Launceston and Northampton)
Scrum-half. Age 22, 5ft 10in, 12st.
Richard, from the Bude area, came to prominence with Launceston. As a student at the Royal Agricultural College, Cirencester, Richard first went to Bath and then to Northampton, where he had a remarkable end to the 1991 season under Wayne Shelford. Very quick over the first few yards, Richard goes through gaps which no one else has seen.

Nancekivell breaks through. Cornwall v. Warwickshire 2.2.91. (*Mike Cox*)

GRAHAM DAWE (Bath)
Hooker. Age 30, 5ft 11in, 13st 10lbs.
Graham, who farms at Milton Abbot just across the Devon border, came to county attention with Launceston and is now in his sixth season with Bath. He played three times for England in 1987 and in Australia in 1988. In the past season he has played for England B and the Barbarians. His throwing-in and power make a tremendous difference to the Cornish pack.

RICHARD KEAST (Redruth)
Tight head prop. Age 25, 6ft, 16st.
A pig farmer in an all-agricultural front row, Richard played senior rugby at seventeen with Newquay Hornets and played his first county championship game a year later. He played for England Colts, but injury, which has dogged his career, prevented him from playing for England Under-23 in 1986.

MARK WESSON (Plymouth Albion)
Lock. Age 27, 6ft 7in, 18st 4lbs.
A commercial designer, Mark had only come back to playing rugby in November 1989. Educated at Newquay, he went on to the University of Southern California where he played water polo. On returning to Newquay he played a few games of rugby for the Hornets before joining Albion. He went on the summer tour of Germany with Cornwall and played ten county games before the final.

A cheerful Mark Wesson awaits his medal. Twickenham 1991. (*John Chapman*)

Opposite: top, Graham Dawe has his fans. Twickenham 1991. (*Mike Cox*)
Bottom, Richard Keast (*right*) with John May, bound for Twickenham after beating Warwickshire.
(*Mike Cox*)

Andy Reed wins the ball. Twickenham 1991. (*Mike Cox*)

ANDY REED (Bath)
Lock. Age 22, 6ft 7ins, 17st 2lbs.
A plant engineer, Andy joined Camborne from Bodmin in 1987/88. He then moved to Plymouth and then to Bath after being invited on their 1990 summer tour. Played for Cornwall Colts, three times for England Colts, and is a wonderful prospect.

Glyn Williams going forward. Twickenham 1991.
(Mike Cox)

GLYN WILLIAMS (Redruth)
Wing forward. Age 27, 6ft 3in, 14st 7lbs.
An electrician, Glyn has played for Cornwall
at all levels from Colts upwards. With forty-
three caps, he took over the captaincy when
Chris Alcock was injured in the final and
inspired the team, saying 'It's destiny, it's
destiny. We will win.'

Adrian Bick on the run. Twickenham 1991. (*Mike Cox*)

ADRIAN BICK (Plymouth Albion)
Wing forward. Age 25, 5ft 11in, 14st 7lbs.
A teacher, Adrian represented Cornwall at schoolboy level upwards and captained the county Under-23s. He played for Penzance-Newlyn before going to college, where he played for both Bath and Lydney before returning to Cornwall.

Jason Atkinson in full flight while Middlesex try a little ballet. Cornwall v. Middlesex 15.12.90. (*John Chapman*)

JASON ATKINSON (St Ives)
No 8. Age 22, 6ft 3in, 14st 10lbs.
A mason, Jason played for Cornwall Colts and the Under-21 side before making his senior début in the game against Gloucestershire at Bristol. He filled the spot previously held by his former clubmate Martin Haag, now with Bath, and is generally rated the find of the season.

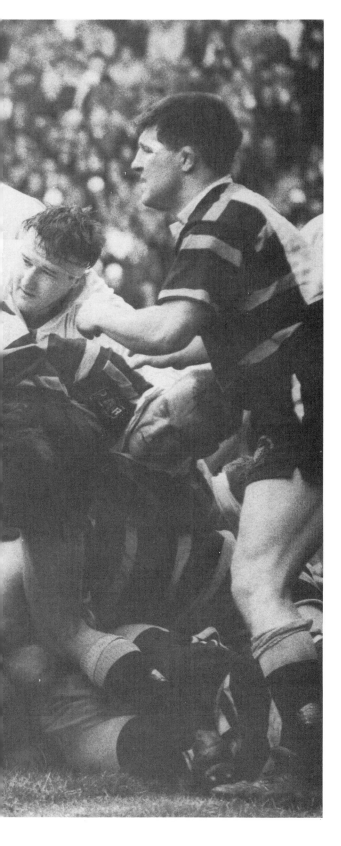

Replacements

MARK CHATTERTON (Exeter)
Wing. Age 28, 6ft 3in, 13st 8lbs.
A school teacher at Taunton, Mark started his club rugby career with Falmouth. He travelled around and played rugby in Australia. He played in two friendlies and was then brought in for semi-final when Tommy Bassett was injured. Shared in the glory when called on to replace Chris Alcock at Twickenham.

Mark Chatterton came on as replacement wing and joined in with the forwards. Twickenham 1991. (*Mike Cox*)

ADAM ELLERY (St Mary's Hospital)
Prop. Age 24, 6ft 1in, 17st.
A final-year medical student, Adam is a great man to have on the bench as he can play on either side and also apply first aid when necessary. Originally from Penzance and Newlyn, he has been unlucky not to play more than eight games for Cornwall but his time will come.

BRIAN ANDREW (Camborne)
Hooker. Age 25, 5ft 10in, 11st 7lbs.
Brian, who runs a pub between Camborne and Redruth, is a very mobile hooker who has played twenty-one times for Cornwall. He has played a vital part in enabling Cornwall to reach Twickenham twice, but has not yet played on the hallowed turf.

PAUL THOMASON (Redruth)
Lock or No 8. Age 29, 6ft 5in, 16st 9lbs.
A miner who has played around three hundred times for his club, Paul is a player with a lot of heart who gave his all in the first two group games.

KEITH PLUMMER (Cleve)
Scrum-half. Age 28, 5ft 8in, 12st 7lbs.
A motor service manager, Keith scored a try in his one Cornwall appearance. He has also played for Bath and Newport.

STUART WHITWORTH (Redruth)
Fly-half. Age 25, 5ft 7in, 12st 10lbs.
A brewery representative, Stuart can play fly-half or centre and has eight Cornwall caps.

10

A Fan's View

One of Cornwall's Army of fans, who attended every county match both home and away, sent me his personal view of the season. I think it is worth recording as it is a non-journalist's version of events.

The season began at St Ives, in bright sunshine with a clear blue sky. The view from the recreation ground, across the bay and looking along the north coast as far as Newquay, was magnificent. Turning around to gaze at the pitch was less inspiring, since Ontario were running a bit too fast and too straight for our boys.

Nonetheless it was an enjoyable afternoon, with the new grandstand full for St Ives' début as a county match venue and the usual splendid hospitality in the clubhouse after the game. My sun-tan improved as well.

We left work early and raced up to Beacon Park, Plymouth, for the Tamar Cup, arriving with just three minutes to spare for a 7 p.m. kick-off. The game didn't start until 7.30. On the bright side, wearing a jumper with the Cornwall 'One and All' logo I was mistaken for an official and allowed free admittance to the ground. The inclusion of Dawe and Reed made a big difference to Cornwall's forwards in an excellent game. Crossed back over the Tamar Bridge with a smile: Devon beaten again.

4 November: Gloucestershire at Bristol.

Decided to travel on the 3rd, breaking the journey at Exeter to view the Pilkington Cup match. Camborne went down with honour; so did a lot of beer upon arrival at Bristol. Like many Cornishmen, I have relatives and friends in the Bristol area and it would have been impolite to refuse their hospitality.

Arrived at Bristol Rugby Ground still feeling the effects of the previous night. A warm, sunny day and a Cornwall win improved my disposition. Both sides threw the ball around, looking to attack at every opportunity. Splendid tries resulted. Unfortunately our defence was as benign as the weather, and the winning margin, 19–10, was narrower than it should have been.

Cornwall's selection for the final friendly against the Royal Navy, under floodlights at St Austell, was reputed to be close to the side which would represent us in the championship. Oh dear! There was some consolation in that several Navy players were eligible for Cornwall. However, the fact was that we were badly beaten by a scratch side drawn mostly from clubs of equivalent or lower standing than our own side. It did not augur well.

Having for years been enthralled at the prowess of Peter Hendy, Chris Durant, Roger Corin and Paul Winnan, among others, it was a sobering thought that none of these stalwarts ever played in a county championship final. So what price the team of 1990–91?

Hope, however, springs eternal, and we began the ADT championship campaign with a long trek to Hertfordshire. Croxley Green wasn't too hard to find, but the pitch was. Even the locals didn't know where it was.

We arrived at the ground just as the officials were setting up their stall at the gate. Two minutes later and we would have been charged £4 entry fee. Talk about a rip-off. Wandering to the far side we discovered the Second XV pitch, where Old Merchant Taylors were playing. The morale of their opponents plummeted when, trailing 22–0, OMTs brought on their coach as a replacement. He was All Black Frank Shelford, who scored immediately from around halfway, traversing the defence like a man wading through treacle.

Back to the main event. Not even a solid turnout of Cornish support, led by the Falmouth Marine Band, could prevent Herts kicking two early penalties. To our relief, Cornwall then got into their stride and ran out comfortable winners. We headed home in good spirits, getting back in time for last orders.

Berkshire. Not a difficult trip, we'd been there before but not in a blizzard. Snow driving horizontally down the pitch as we arrived to be informed the game was off. Committee men took pity and offered food and drink, not realizing coachloads were pulling into the car park. Within minutes the committee buffet was gone. Collected a programme for the match. I have seen many games without a programme, but this was my first programme without a match. A marathon trip back to the Duchy was finally concluded some time after midnight. It was probably a good decision not to play the game in the snow: the match ball was white.

Even the devout were unsure of our chances against Middlesex. A good-sized

crowd at Redruth got behind Cornwall and after a cautious start we turned in a superb display of fiery second-phase work. Middlesex simply could not cope. It brought back memories of 1967 and 1969 when Cornwall routed teams who, on paper, should have beaten us comfortably. It was the heart and commitment of the Cornwall team which stood out, and for the first time we repaired to the bar thinking we might go to Twickenham . . . and maybe win there.

January, and the second trip to Newbury. The wind was even stronger than last time, the showers torrential and conditions muddy. Just the time to get a seat in the grandstand. Or it would have been, but the grandstand roof had been taken down because of the fierce wind.

The huge supermarket car park opposite filled to capacity as the Cornish supporters filled the spaces. The Tesco manager, obviously no rugby man, sent out staff to try to evict Cornish vehicles. By this time several supporters' coaches had arrived and, unable to park or turn around, blocked the store's access and caused a tailback on to the road. Chaos.

The match itself was memorable for the refereeing. Cornwall's forwards were hugely superior and Berkshire never looked like scoring, even with the referee's help. Four tries were awarded to Cornwall and a further six disallowed by the referee who was probably the only person in the ground not to see the ball touched down.

We dominated up front so much in the semi-final with Warwickshire that there was no call for nail-biting at the end. More and more merchandise – caps, scarves and rosettes – was evident on the terraces. One had the feeling that Twickeham was going to see the greatest Cornish invasion yet.

Yorkshire's classy outsides had us all worried about the final, but their supporters were no match for Cornwall either in numbers or inventiveness. Never before had there been such an array of black and gold. Choughs, bananas, 'Obby 'Osses, pantomime animals and enormous replica pasties were on parade in the main street. The Marine Band marched across a dual carriageway, bringing both lanes to a standstill.

Five hours before the kick-off and Waterloo Station was already dominated by Cornish scarves and rosettes. We were looking for the Twickenham train. A small group headed for platform 16 and the rest began to follow. The man at the front admitted, 'This is the first time I've been to London without getting lost.' It turned out the train from platform 16 was going to Southampton, but fortunately we were redirected to the correct platform.

Much has already been written about the remarkable match, and the influence of the massive Cornish support. It was certainly a good natured crowd, incurring the displeasure only of the groundsman as the after-match celebrations spilled on to the pitch. Even the stewards seemed to enter into the spirit of things.

Travelling home on Sunday morning there were Cornish cars and supporters all the way, returning home on Census Day. Arriving in Truro just before the victorious team it was a privilege to see the reception outside the City Hall.

As the crowd began to disperse, the comment was made, 'How are we going to top this?' The answer came back, 'This is only the rehearsal – wait for next year.' It will be worth waiting for.

Friendly rivals, it was that sort of day. Yorkshireman Allan Woodward tells Cornwall supporter Peter Reddy who is going to win. (*John Chapman*)

Previous page: The party starts on the pitch. Twickenham 1991. (*John Chapman*)

Grant Champion gets steamed up after the Warwickshire victory. Cornwall v. Warwickshire 2.2.91. (*Mike Cox*)

What the People Said

One of rugby's most senior statesmen, Mickey Steele-Bodger, said, 'It was one of the great days of my life at Twickenham. I am privileged to say I was there.' A former England flanker, chairman of selectors and chairman of the International Rugby Board, Mr Steele-Bodger added, 'It was a superb spectacle and I am delighted the Cornish support got what it deserved. At the end of the day there was only one side in it. I have to pay great respect to the pack, especially the two second rows ... Cornwall won because they had heart. It all turned on heart and the spirit of the support. I was thrilled for them.'

Mr David Roberts, chairman of Cornwall County Council, had predicted a high scoring game with Cornwall winning by 10 points. 'Everyone has their own special memories, like the moment when the Falmouth Marine Band came on to the pitch, the sight of a 5-feet-long Cornish pasty hanging from the crossbar. We all remember the superb fight back in the last quarter, every metre gained got a louder cheer than England winning the Grand Slam. It was a team effort, a great fight back showing the very spirit of Cornishness.'

Centre Grant Champion, whose conversion attempt would have won the game after eighty minutes, 'If I'd had a gun at that moment I would have shot myself.'

Winger Tony Mead said Glyn Williams, who took over as skipper, had been inspiring in extra time: 'Glyn said "We can't let these people down." He kept telling us "It's Destiny, It's Destiny, It's Destiny." We will win. I think nearly all of us had a tear in our eye at that moment.'

Coach Benjie Thomas, soaking up the euphoria after the game, said, 'It was unbelievable. When we got our first try I thought it was going to be simply a consolation. In extra time our forwards took them apart. You couldn't pick out anyone, they were all unbelievable.'

Mike Trott, the Cornwall RFU president: 'Those who were there will remember it for the rest of their lives. When the chips were down and we went into extra time it was the spirit, the will to win and above all the fitness which saw us through. Benjie Thomas brought us a team with the physical and mental fitness to win the championship which had eluded us for eighty-three years.'

Cornwall selector Don Palmer: 'It was The Great Escape.'

Cornwall prop John May: 'Now I believe in reincarnation.'

Glyn Williams celebrates with wife, Jenny (*right*), and the coach's daughter, Helen.
Twickenham 1991. (*Mike Cox*)

Final Thoughts

The ticket sales for the Cornwall – Yorkshire game were £370,000, easily a record in a competition which had attracted just 7,000 to Twickenham the previous year. The two finalist counties received just £8,000 each, while all other counties in the competition received £6,000. Cornwall received another £20,000 as their percentage of ticket sales in the county, but their expenses in kitting out the squad and preparing them for the final totalled around £14,000. 'They were looked after better than the England team,' said treasurer Ray Plummer.

* * *

It is not often a journalist gets the opportunity to praise colleagues on rival newspapers or in other branches of the media, so I am pleased to be able to do so. The Cornwall rugby team, without any doubt, gets more exposure and coverage than any other county side in the land and the supporters who have not been able to get to matches have been fortunate, in some instances, to be able to both watch them live on television and, for every match, to hear live commentary on the radio. The BBC Radio Cornwall commentaries of Gerry Clarke and Dave Martin have been exceptional, bringing home not just the action but all the emotion which goes with Cornish rugby.

TSW became the first station to televise a county championship match live when they showed the semi-final. They gave an excellent service to the Cornish fans, and wanted to follow this up with full coverage of the final. However, the BBC had the rights at Twickenham and, after an eleventh-hour decision, BBC South West showed the whole match live. They certainly ended up with the scoop of the century in terms of interest in Cornwall.

Some people recorded the match on video and have viewed it over forty times. A friend of mine took the video to Switzerland where he and another Cornishman were in tears as they watched it. The recording of that match has gone all over the world, and I will put into print a heartfelt thanks from Cornish supporters to those who organized the coverage.

The press in Cornwall have also given the game tremendous coverage, in bad times as well as good. As well as the *Western Morning News* and the *Evening Herald* I am happy to single out Paul Bawden, of the Packet series, a former chairman of the Cornwall selectors with a passionate interest in the game, and Gerald Phillipps, of the *West Briton*. Gerald retired after the final and his colleagues, including picture editor Paul Roberts, produced a wonderful front-page collage of pictures of the Cornwall team with the headline 'We did it for you Gerald!'

* * *

Tommy Bassett, blood still dripping from his ear, with his wife, Sian, and parents, Eddie and Daphne Bassett. Twickenham 1991. (*Mike Cox*)

After Cornwall lost to Durham in the 1989 final, hooker Graham Dawe was back at Twickenham just two weeks later playing for Bath in the Pilkington Cup final against Leicester. This time he was on the winning side, and Bath beat Leicester, for whom the legendary Dusty Hare was playing his last game.

The following season Dawe was in the Pilkington final again, scoring a try when Bath trounced Gloucester.

In the 1991 season it was Richard Nancekivell's honour to appear in the two finals. He had made a remarkable leap to the top at Northampton under All-Black Wayne Shelford, coming into the side in the semi-final and holding his place for the final against Harlequins.

Unfortunately dreams did not come true twice, and despite a valiant display by him and his Northampton colleagues they eventually went down in extra time.

*   *   *

Tommy Bassett announced his retirement from the county game right after the final. 'Nothing can ever beat this,' he said. 'I was lucky to get back into the team what with the accidents I have had and my age being against me. Now I am happy to retire from county rugby.' The Duke of Edinburgh shook hands with all the team when they received their tankards and when it came to Tommy he asked about the blood coming from his ear. 'It's still there, I think,' Tommy reassured him.

*   *   *